Fabulous Fairholme

Breakfasts & Brunches

Copyright © 2007 Sylvia Main
Food Preparation and Styling: Sunny Dinney
Editor: Sue Frause
Food and Inn Photography: John Archer
Inn and Garden Photography: Cathie Ferguson
Book Design and Layout: Reber Creative

Printed and bound in Canada by Friesens Printing

Library and Archives Canada Cataloguing in Publication

Main, Sylvia
    Fabulous Fairholme : breakfasts & brunches : recipes from the award-winning historic Fairholme Manor Inn, Victoria, BC / by Sylvia Main.

Includes index.
ISBN 978-0-9783169-0-7

    1. Breakfasts. 2. Brunches. 3. Fairholme Manor.
I. Fairholme Manor II. Title.

TX733.M375 2007   641.5'2   C2007-901669-3

Published by Fairholme Manor Inc.

To order copies, please contact:

Fairholme Manor Inn
638 Rockland Place
Victoria, BC
Canada   V8S 3R2
Phone: (250) 598-3240
Fax: (250) 598-3299

www.fairholmemanor.com

Fabulous Fairholme

Breakfasts & Brunches

To my beautiful daughters Simone and Nicola,
whom I love more than anything.
And to my adorable husband Roscoe for
all his support, patience and true love.

Fairholme Manor is situated in the lush Rockland area of Victoria, British Columbia on Vancouver Island. The Italianate-style home was built in 1885 by Dr. John C. Davie, a medical pioneer and long-term provincial health officer. Fairholme Manor is located adjacent to the gardens of Government House, the official residence of the Lieutenant Governor of British Columbia, the Queen's representative. Queen Elizabeth II and Prince Phillip, Duke of Edinburgh paid a visit to Government House in 2002.

Accolades

Canada Select 5 Star Accommodation 2006 and 2007

"2006 Grand Award Winner for Best Canadian Bed and Breakfast of the Year," *Andrew Harper's Hideaway Report*

"Highly Recommended," *Fodor's* Vancouver and British Columbia Edition 2006

Featured in *Karen Brown's Pacific Northwest: Exceptional Places to Stay & Itineraries*

Recipes featured in *Glamour* magazine, May 2002

Featured in Bill Gleesen's *Weekends for Two in the Pacific Northwest*

Recipes

Acknowledgements

This cookbook would not have been possible without the support of my family, friends and wonderful guests. My deepest gratitude to:

My loyal staff, who treat the Inn as their own. A special thanks to my assistant and talented chef Sunny Dinney, who makes everything delicious and so much fun!

My mother, for her ongoing love and support.

John Archer, who photographed us at the crack of dawn and made our food look so tantalizing.

Cathie Ferguson, who has been photographing Fairholme Manor from the beginning. Her pictures are lovely.

Inge Ranzinger, for all the great recipes and her art that adorns Fairholme.

Sarah Thompson, who is like a daughter to me and is dedicated to Fairholme.

Beth von Hebel, for her competence and heart of gold.

Claudette Roddier, for her classic French cooking skills and beautiful food.

All my cooks over the years, including Janet Thompson, Tina Tulloch and Cara Johnson. This book is a collaboration of recipes from all these talented young women.

Sandy Reber of Reber Creative; Gerhard Aichelberger of Friesens; Deirdre Campbell of Tartan Public Relations.

My wonderful friend and brilliant editor Sue Frause, for her constant support and belief in me over the years.

Introduction

Fairholme Manor has gained a worldwide reputation for its memorable breakfasts and brunches since it opened in 1999.

Over the years, we have had numerous requests from guests and friends to create a book filled with our favourite recipes and ideas. As a result, I collaborated with my talented team and produced a cookbook that contains recipes that are both tasty and easy to make. Plus, they have been tested time and again in Fairholme's kitchen, and they really work!

I've always felt that a homemade breakfast or brunch is the ideal way to start a busy day or relaxing weekend. Fresh, quality foods are key ingredients in all our recipes – including organic dairy and meats. We are fortunate to have a bountiful herb and vegetable garden, a wide variety of edible flowers and free range eggs from Maureen our "Egg Lady." So tasty!

As a child growing up in Austria, some of my fondest memories are the trips I made with my family to local farms. There we would get fresh fruits and vegetables, along with farm fresh eggs. I spent many hours in the kitchen with my mother, who introduced me to her flair for entertaining in style.

Although I have no formal training as a chef, I'm passionate about food. With assistance from my talented team of creative cooks, I've gained an invaluable insight into food preparation and presentation. This book is filled with yummy recipes and beautiful photographs of the breakfasts and brunches we serve at Fairholme Manor. They are a reflection of the casual comfort and chic European style of our Inn.

I hope you will be inspired by this book to create some of our tasty breakfasts and brunches in your own home. They are meant to be shared with family and friends.

Enjoy *Fabulous Fairholme!*

Sylvia Main

Foreword

As a travel writer, I sleep around a lot.

Whether it's a small bed and breakfast, an urban boutique hotel or a four-star resort – I've stayed in some wonderful hostelries around the world.

Fairholme Manor is one of my favourites.

Part of the magic of Fairholme is that it fits any occasion. Whether it's a solo retreat, a girls' getaway or a stolen weekend with my husband – the Inn always feels right, no matter what the reason.

The ingredients that make it all so delightful are carefully crafted by Sylvia. From her cheery welcome at the front door to her animated conversation while serving one of the Inn's legendary breakfasts, her zest for life is contagious.

Fabulous Fairholme is more than a cookbook – it's a lifestyle book. Inside are recipes and photographs that capture the essence of Sylvia's lovely Inn.

It's a book to sit down with over a cup of tea.

It's a book to share with a friend.

Pretty fabulous, indeed.

Sue Frause

Sue Frause, editor

BAKED GRAPEFRUIT

SERVES 2

1	whole grapefruit
2 tablespoons	maple syrup or brown sugar

Slice grapefruit in half and de-seed. Run a sharp knife around inside edges of rind and slice fruit into sections. Do not remove. Pour 1 tablespoon syrup or brown sugar over the centre of each grapefruit half. Place on a baking sheet lined with parchment paper and broil for about 5 minutes or until edges turn brown. Serve warm.

FAIRHOLME GRANOLA

3 cups	large rolled oats
1 cup	wheat bran
½ cup	wheat germ
½ cup	oat bran
1 cup	unsweetened coconut
½ teaspoon	salt
½ cup	sesame seeds
½ cup	pumpkin seeds
½ cup	sunflower seeds
1 cup	almonds, sliced
2 tablespoons	cinnamon
½ cup	sunflower oil
¼ cup	water
1 cup	maple syrup
2 teaspoons	pure vanilla
1 cup	dried cranberries
½ cup	dried apricots, diced

This crunchy granola recipe is foolproof. It is delicious served with creamy vanilla yogurt. Guests have been requesting this recipe for years.

Preheat oven to 250°F and line two large baking sheets with parchment paper.

In a large bowl combine the first 11 ingredients. Mix well. In a separate bowl combine oil, water, maple syrup and vanilla. Add to the dry ingredients and mix thoroughly.

Divide the granola between the two baking sheets and pack down over the entire sheet. Bake for about 1½ hours, stirring every 15 minutes. The granola should be golden brown and crunchy when done. Allow it to cool and then add dried fruit. Store in airtight container.

VANILLA BERRY PARFAIT

This makes an elegant breakfast offering that's quick and easy to prepare. Layer Fairholme Granola (page 17) with rich vanilla yogurt, fresh berries or other seasonal fruit into individual serving glasses. Serve immediately.

FRUIT MUESLI

SERVES 4 – 6

4 cups	quick oats
2 tablespoons	maple syrup
1 cup	milk
¼ cup	water
2 teaspoons	cinnamon
2 cups	plain or vanilla yogurt
2	large apples or pears, peeled and grated
2 tablespoons	wheat germ
juice	½ lemon

This very healthy breakfast is easy to assemble and can be prepared the night before.

The night before:

Stir together oats, maple syrup, milk, water and cinnamon and put into refrigerator overnight.

In the morning:

Add yogurt, grated apples or pears, and all other ingredients into the muesli and serve with fresh berries or diced dried fruit.

MELON REFRESHER

MAKES 4 SERVINGS

2 cups	watermelon, cut into 1" cubes
1	small ripe honeydew or cantaloupe (optional), cut into 1" cubes
2 tablespoons	lime juice
2 tablespoons	honey
1 tablespoon	fresh mint, finely chopped

Remove skin from melons. Dice the flesh into 1" cubes and place in a mixing bowl. Squeeze lime juice over melons and thoroughly mix in honey and fresh mint. Serve chilled.

This refreshing fruit salad is wonderful in the summer using only watermelon and plenty of mint. To make the salad more elegant, use a melon baller to shape fruit. Garnish with fresh mint leaves.

LEMON RICOTTA PANCAKES

SERVES 4 – 6

5 eggs	separated
zest	1 large lemon or orange
1 cup	milk
1¾ cups	ricotta cheese
1 cup	all-purpose flour, sifted
2½ teaspoons	baking powder
½ cup	sugar
dash	salt
	maple syrup and/or crème fraîche

Preheat griddle or skillet on medium heat.

Mix the egg yolks. Sift and mix the dry ingredients and combine with egg yolks, lemon or orange zest, milk and ricotta cheese.

Beat the egg whites until stiff. Gently fold into the egg-ricotta batter. Lightly oil griddle and pour a pancake-sized amount onto griddle with a ½ cup measuring scoop. Cook until bubbles form. Flip and cook other side until golden.

Serve with warm maple syrup and/or crème fraîche.

This soufflé style pancake will melt in your mouth. Flip only once and don't flatten the pancake after flipping. This keeps it nice and light. Many guests phone ahead to make sure we'll be serving these pancakes during their stay.

FAIRHOLME CRÊPES

SERVES 6 – 8

1 cup	all-purpose flour, sifted
2	large eggs
1 cup	milk
dash	salt
2 teaspoons	sugar (if using sweet filling, otherwise omit)
1 tablespoon	vegetable oil or melted butter

To prevent crêpes from sticking together, stack crêpes on top of each other separated by pieces of parchment paper. This makes it easy to prepare crêpes in advance and store in refrigerator until ready to use.

Whisk together above ingredients until smooth. Place in refrigerator for at least 1 hour or overnight.

Heat lightly oiled, non-stick skillet or crêpe pan over medium heat.

Pour 1 medium ladle of batter into pan and swirl to cover entire pan. Cook briefly and flip over with a wide spatula. Continue to cook until golden for about 1-2 minutes. Make sure that the pan comes back up to temperature between crêpes.

At Fairholme we use the classic method and simply fill the crêpes with a tablespoon of homemade apricot, strawberry or raspberry jam and sprinkle them with a dusting of powdered sugar.

APRICOT GINGER JAM

6 SMALL JARS

4½ cups	fresh, ripe apricots
1 tablespoon	fresh ginger, minced
¼ cup	lemon juice, freshly squeezed
7½ cups	sugar
2 packs	pectin powder

Peel and pit the apricots, chop fine. In large, heavy pot add apricots, ginger, lemon juice and sugar. Bring to a boil for 1 minute over high heat, stirring constantly. Remove from heat and stir in pectin. Stir jam for 5 minutes while skimming off foam. Pour jam into sterilized jars, seal and store in refrigerator or cool place.

This jam tastes like it's fresh from the tree. Peaches or plums may be substituted for the apricots. It's delicious spread inside fresh crêpes. Sprinkle with powdered sugar.

RASPBERRY VANILLA JAM

8 SMALL JARS

5 cups	fresh or frozen raspberries
7 cups	sugar
1	fresh vanilla bean, cut in half and scraped
1½ pack	pectin powder *(use 2 packs of pectin for frozen berries)*

Wash and crush raspberries with potato masher. In large, heavy-bottomed pot add berries, sugar and vanilla bean. Bring to a boil over high heat, stirring constantly. Boil for 1 minute.

Remove from heat and stir in pectin. Stir jam for 5 minutes while skimming off foam. Remove vanilla bean pod. Pour jam into sterilized jars, seal and store in refrigerator or cool place.

Blueberries, loganberries, strawberries or blackberries may be substituted for the raspberries.

SAVOURY BREAKFAST CRÊPE FILLING

SERVES 8

16	large eggs
½ cup	light cream
16-20	medium mushrooms
2 bunches	spinach
¼ cup	cream cheese
1 cup	cheddar cheese, grated
2-4 tablespoons	chives and/or basil, finely chopped
1 teaspoon	salt
dash	cayenne and black pepper
½ cup	butter
8	crêpes (page 26)

Sauté mushrooms in about 5 tablespoons butter until lightly browned.

Sauté spinach in about 3 tablespoons butter until wilted. Do not overcook.

Here is how we prepare crêpes for two in the morning:

Place a crêpe on each plate and set in 250°F oven.

Heat 1 tablespoon butter in skillet. Add 4 beaten eggs and a splash of cream, then scramble until it begins to set. Add 1 tablespoon cream cheese, 1 teaspoon chives and/or basil, cayenne, salt and pepper to taste. Add about 3 tablespoons each of the spinach and mushrooms. Keep stirring until lightly scrambled. Do not overcook. Eggs should still be moist.

Remove crêpes from oven and place filling into the middle of each one. Fold over from each side, forming into a log and sprinkle with grated cheddar cheese and return to oven for another 3-5 minutes.

Remove from oven. Sprinkle entire plate with finely chopped chives or parsley.

Repeat for additional servings.

BLUEBERRY PANCAKES

SERVES 4 – 6

2 cups	all-purpose flour
2 teaspoons	baking powder
1 teaspoon	baking soda
3 tablespoons	sugar
pinch	salt
2	large eggs, lightly beaten
zest	1 large lemon or orange
3 cups	buttermilk
4 tablespoons	unsalted butter, melted
1 cup	fresh or frozen blueberries
	maple syrup

At Fairholme, we mix in a dash of cinnamon with our powdered sugar for added flavour.

Preheat griddle or skillet on medium heat.

Sift together flour, baking powder, baking soda, sugar and salt in a bowl. Stir until thoroughly mixed and make a well in the centre. In a separate bowl, whisk together eggs, lemon or orange zest, buttermilk and melted butter. Pour mixture into centre of well and gently fold together. The batter should have a pebbly or slightly lumpy consistency.

Coat the griddle with vegetable oil. Pour about ½ cup batter onto the heated griddle, about 2" apart. Scatter 8 to 10 blueberries on top of each pancake. When bubbles begin to appear on top, carefully flip over each pancake and continue to cook until golden brown.

Sprinkle with powdered sugar and serve warm with maple syrup and butter.

FAIRHOLME'S EGGS BENEDICT

SERVES 4

Eggs Benedict is such an elegant breakfast dish and is much easier to prepare than you may think. It's perfect for weekends, when company is coming or for special occasions.

8	large poached eggs (page 69)
4	English muffins
8 slices	Canadian bacon
8 slices	tomato
1 cup	mixed salad greens (optional)
2 tablespoons	chives or parsley, finely chopped
	cayenne
	butter
	Hollandaise Sauce (page 38)

Prepare Hollandaise Sauce and set aside. Lightly toast and butter English muffins, keep warm in oven. Heat Canadian bacon in skillet with a little butter, do not brown. Place in oven with English muffins.

Poach eggs and remove excess water. To assemble, place English muffin on plate. Top with Canadian bacon, greens, tomato slice and poached egg. Pour 1-2 tablespoons Hollandaise Sauce over each egg. Garnish with chopped herbs and a pinch of cayenne.

Variations

We offer our guests several variations of this wonderful dish. Substitute the Canadian bacon with fresh smoked salmon or smoked tuna. For a vegetarian option, wilt fresh spinach in a little butter with minced garlic and season with salt and pepper. Flavourful summer heirloom tomatoes are another way to spice up this classic dish.

BLENDER HOLLANDAISE

SERVES 6

3	egg yolks
2 tablespoons	lemon juice
pinch	cayenne
¼ teaspoon	salt
¾ cup	butter

This recipe works every time and is a cinch to prepare.

Melt butter in microwave. Place egg yolks, lemon juice, cayenne and salt in blender and turn on high for about 10 seconds.

With blender running, pour the melted butter into the egg mixture in a slow, steady stream.

Allow the butter to fully incorporate and blend for 30 more seconds. The sauce should be light, creamy and smooth. Serve immediately.

BREAKFAST CHEESE SOUFFLÉ

SERVES 6

8 slices	thick white bread with crusts removed, cubed
1 cup	sharp cheddar cheese, grated
5	eggs
2½ cups	whole milk
2 teaspoons	Dijon mustard
dash	cayenne
½ teaspoon	salt and pepper
4 tablespoons	finely diced chives

This savoury breakfast dish is perfect with cold smoked salmon or crispy bacon.

Generously butter 6 ramekins, then layer bread and cheese evenly in each one. Whisk together eggs, milk, Dijon mustard, cayenne, salt, pepper and chives. Pour over bread mixture.

Cover tightly and put in refrigerator overnight. The next morning, bake at 450°F for 35-40 minutes or until soufflés are puffy and golden. Serve immediately.

ASIAGO AND GREEN ONION OMELETTE

SERVES 2

4	large eggs
¼ cup	water
	fleur de sel and freshly ground pepper (optional)
½ teaspoon	butter
½ teaspoon	vegetable oil
½ cup	Asiago cheese, grated
2	green onions

Heat butter and oil in a 10" non-stick skillet.

Vigorously whisk eggs, water, salt and pepper in a large bowl. Try to keep as much air incorporated in the egg mixture as possible. Pour half the egg mixture into the skillet and let sit for about 30 seconds.

Using a silicone spatula, gently pull cooked egg mixture toward the centre and away from the edges of the pan. Lightly swirl raw egg mixture toward the outside of the pan. When the centre is thickened and egg is barely moist, sprinkle Asiago and green onion evenly onto the omelette.

Use spatula to lift one edge and gently fold omelette in half. Turn heat to low and continue to cook for 30 more seconds. Holding warmed plate in one hand, gently tilt the skillet and slide omelette onto the plate. Garnish with finely sliced green onions.

Repeat for second omelette.

OMELETTE VARIATIONS

Spinach, Mushroom and Gruyère with Bacon Omelette

Wash and roughly chop 1 cup baby spinach. Slice 4 mushrooms and sauté lightly in butter with salt and pepper. Set aside. Cook 2 pieces of bacon until crisp and grate ¼ cup Gruyère cheese. Crumble bacon, combine with other ingredients, and divide mixture between omelettes. Season with salt and pepper.

Fresh Basil, Cherry Tomato and Mozzarella Omelette

Wash and quarter 8 cherry tomatoes. Finely chop 1 tablespoon fresh basil and grate ¼ cup mozzarella. Divide mixture evenly among omelettes and season with salt and pepper.

Asparagus, Prosciutto and Parmesan Omelette

Blanch 10 asparagus tips. Cut two pieces of prosciutto widthwise into thin ribbons. Grate a scant ¼ cup fresh Parmesan cheese. Place asparagus and prosciutto into a bowl and toss with 1 tablespoon olive oil and a dash of coarse salt and pepper. Divide between omelettes and sprinkle with Parmesan cheese.

EGG BLOSSOMS

SERVES 6

4 sheets	phyllo pastry
2 tablespoons	butter, melted
4 teaspoons	Parmesan cheese, grated
4	eggs
2	green onions and/or fresh basil, finely chopped
	salt, pepper and cayenne to taste
	butter for greasing tins

Egg Blossoms are very easy to make and look impressive on the plate. Serve with bacon or sausage.

Preheat oven to 425°F.

Brush sheet of phyllo with melted butter. Top with another sheet and brush with butter. Cut stack into six 4" squares. Repeat with remaining 2 sheets. Stack 3 squares together so corners do not overlap. Press into buttered muffin tins.

Sprinkle Parmesan cheese into each phyllo-lined tin. Break 1 egg into each tin. Sprinkle with green onion and/or fresh basil, salt, pepper and cayenne.

Bake 15-20 minutes. Pastry should be golden and eggs fully cooked. Serve with Sundried Tomato Sauce.

Sundried Tomato Sauce

Place ¾ cup preserved sundried tomatoes into a blender and pulse until mixture is smooth. Add 2 tablespoons warm water and blend well. Add salt and pepper to taste.

POPPY SEED BREAD CUPS WITH SCRAMBLED EGGS

SERVES 2

2 slices	whole wheat sandwich bread, crusts removed
	butter, softened
1 tablespoon	Dijon mustard
1 teaspoon	poppy seeds
1 recipe	Perfect Scrambled Eggs (page 60)
	fresh herbs and dash cayenne

Preheat oven to 350°F.

Remove crust from bread. Butter both sides and spread Dijon mustard on one side. With mustard side facing up, lightly press into extra large muffin tin. Sprinkle with poppy seeds.

Bake in oven for about 20 minutes. Remove bread "cups" from muffin tin and place on warmed plate. Fill cups with Perfect Scrambled Eggs. Eggs should spill slightly out of each bread cup onto one side of the plate. Garnish with fresh herbs and cayenne.

Fairholme guests love this dish served with fresh pork or turkey sausages on the side. This recipe is simple to make but very dramatic.

ZUCCHINI OREGANO FRITTATA

SERVES 6

8	large eggs
3	additional egg whites
½ cup	milk
1 cup	feta cheese, crumbled
½ cup	ricotta cheese
½ teaspoon	salt
½ teaspoon	ground black pepper
1 tablespoon	olive oil
2	medium zucchini, cut into small cubes
1 cup	button mushrooms, sliced
2 cloves	garlic, finely chopped
2 teaspoons	fresh oregano or basil, chopped
pinch	cayenne
¼ cup	Parmesan cheese, grated

Preheat oven to broil.

In mixing bowl whisk together eggs, egg whites, milk, feta cheese, ricotta cheese, salt and pepper.

Heat oil in large ovenproof skillet on medium high heat and sauté mushrooms for 3 minutes. Add zucchini and continue to cook until tender. Add garlic and oregano and cook for 1 more minute.

Pour egg mixture over zucchini and mushrooms in pan. Use a spatula to fold egg mixture under sides of frittata as if making an omelette. Do not stir. This should take 3-4 minutes.

While centre is still moist sprinkle generously with Parmesan cheese. Place in oven under broiler until frittata puffs up and the cheese is lightly browned. Give the pan a little shake to ensure the egg is set in the middle. Remove from oven and cut into wedges.

Tastes delicious served with smoked salmon.

BACON, CHEESE AND TOMATO FRITTATA

SERVES 6

4 slices	bacon
12	large eggs
½ cup	milk
1	small green onion, chopped
1	tomato, chopped
2 teaspoons	Dijon mustard
¾ cup	cream cheese
¼ cup	fresh basil, finely chopped
½ teaspoon	salt
¼ teaspoon	black pepper
¼ teaspoon	cayenne

For a more elegant look, prepare frittatas in well-greased individual ramekins or large muffin tins.

Topping

2 tablespoons	Parmesan cheese, grated
1	tomato

Cook bacon in skillet until almost crisp. Drain on paper towel and set aside. Whisk together eggs, milk, green onion, tomato, Dijon mustard, cream cheese and basil. Season with salt, pepper and cayenne.

Add cooked bacon bits to egg mixture and pour into well-greased 10" pie plate or ramekins. The frittata may be prepared up to this point and then sealed and refrigerated until morning.

Bake in 350°F oven for about 30 minutes or until puffy around the edges and a tester comes out clean.

Slice the remaining tomato and arrange it on top of the frittata. Sprinkle with Parmesan or Romano cheese and place under the broiler for 4 minutes.

Serve immediately.

TOMATO AND SPINACH STRATA WITH ASIAGO

SERVES 12

10 slices	French bread, cut into 1" cubes
8	eggs
2 cups	whole milk
1 cup	ricotta cheese
1 tablespoon	Dijon mustard
dash	Worcestershire sauce
½ teaspoon	cayenne
1 teaspoon	salt
1 teaspoon	freshly ground pepper
4 cups	fresh spinach
3	Roma tomatoes, sliced
½ cup	Asiago cheese, grated

Strata is an ideal brunch dish for overnight guests. It can be prepared the night before and baked in the morning. Serve with whole wheat toast and cold smoked salmon, sausages or Canadian bacon on the side.

Preheat oven to 350°F.

Grease a 9"x13" glass baking dish with butter. Place cubes of French bread in dish to completely cover bottom. Sprinkle bread with half of the Asiago cheese.

Place spinach evenly over bread and cheese. Whisk together eggs, milk, ricotta cheese, Dijon mustard, Worcestershire sauce, cayenne, salt and pepper. Pour mixture over the spinach layer.

Place sliced tomatoes evenly on top and sprinkle with remaining Asiago cheese. Cover dish tightly and refrigerate overnight.

Bake strata uncovered for 1 hour. Let stand 10 minutes before serving.

ROASTED BABY POTATOES

SERVES 4 – 6

24	small new potatoes, halved
2 tablespoons	each butter and olive oil
	salt and ground pepper to taste
dash	paprika
1 tablespoon	freshly chopped parsley, chives or rosemary

Wash and halve new potatoes.

Place halved potatoes in pot of cold, salted water. Bring to boil. When the water reaches a boil, strain potatoes and let steam dry. Potatoes should not be fully cooked.

Heat butter and oil mixture in heavy skillet on high heat. Add potatoes to hot pan and stir well to coat with butter/oil.

Add salt, pepper and paprika. If using rosemary, add now. Continue to cook for about 10 minutes until potatoes turn nice and brown in the pan.

Sprinkle with fresh herbs of your choice.

The key to perfect roasted potatoes that don't mush up is to undercook them during the boiling process. And don't be afraid to use high heat when frying them. They will brown to perfection!

SMOKED SALMON AND BAGELS WITH LEMON CREAM

SERVES 6

6	bagels (plain, poppy seed or whole wheat)
8 ounces	wild smoked salmon
1 cup	cream cheese
1 teaspoon	lemon zest
4 tablespoons	red onion, very finely chopped
	fleur de sel
	fresh ground pepper
1 tablespoon	olive oil
	fresh chives for garnish, finely chopped

Place cream cheese and lemon zest in bowl and mix at high speed for 1 minute or until smooth. Lightly toast bagels.

Divide cream cheese mixture evenly and spread on bagels. Top each half with smoked salmon and place halves on plates.

Sprinkle each bagel with red onion, a pinch of fleur de sel and ground pepper.

Garnish with chopped chives and a drizzle of olive oil.

For brunch, serve with Perfect Scrambled Eggs (page 60).

ZUCCHINI FRITTERS

SERVES 4

2	medium zucchini, grated
3	eggs, lightly beaten
¼ cup	milk
¼ cup	cream cheese
½ cup	all-purpose flour
1 teaspoon	salt
½ teaspoon	black pepper
4 tablespoons	fresh parsley, finely chopped
2 tablespoons	chopped chives
	cayenne to taste
	vegetable oil (for frying)

Delicious with sour cream. Wow your guests by using fritters as a base for Eggs Benedict or as an alternative to English muffins.

Preheat oven to 350°F.

Grate zucchini into bowl. Add all other ingredients and mix well.

Heat oil in large skillet over medium heat. When oil is hot, drop very large tablespoons full of the mixture into the pan. Adjust heat. You want the fritters to cook slowly and evenly.

Flip and continue cooking on other side, about 3 minutes per side. Place fritters on baking sheet lined with parchment paper and bake in oven for 6 minutes. Fritters will puff up slightly. Serve immediately.

PERFECT SCRAMBLED EGGS

SERVES 2

It is very important to keep the temperature low when scrambling eggs. The end result is an incredibly moist and fluffy egg.

6	eggs
½ cup	light cream
¾ teaspoon	salt
pinch	cayenne
1 tablespoon	butter
	freshly chopped herbs for garnish (chives, tarragon, parsley)

Crack eggs into mixing bowl. Add cream, salt and cayenne. Heat a non-stick skillet over medium low heat. Add butter to pan. Whisk eggs vigorously for 2 minutes to incorporate air into mixture.

Pour egg mixture into preheated skillet. Slowly cook the eggs using a spatula to gently fold raw egg under. Don't rush or "stir" the eggs. When eggs are almost cooked yet still moist, remove from heat. Fold eggs one more time and let the residual heat from pan continue cooking the eggs.

Sprinkle with freshly chopped herbs. Serve immediately.

We often serve these scrambled eggs with a side of chilled, fresh smoked salmon or smoked tuna, fresh tomato salsa (page 62), and whole grain toast. The ingredients and colours of the warm fluffy scrambled eggs, cold fish, tangy tomato salsa and crunchy toast are a perfect match.

Breakfasts & Brunches

TOMATO SALSA

Cherry or regular tomatoes may be used in this salsa. Heirloom tomatoes are particularly tasty when they're in season.

This salsa showcases bright red tomatoes and fresh herbs that everyone enjoys. For a more colourful salsa, use a combination of yellow and red tomatoes.

2 cups	tomatoes
½	red onion, finely chopped
2 cloves	minced garlic
1 tablespoon	balsamic vinegar
1 tablespoon	olive oil
3 tablespoons	chopped fresh basil
1 teaspoon	salt
1 teaspoon	brown sugar
juice	½ lime
	fresh ground pepper

Quarter cherry tomatoes or dice larger tomatoes into small pieces. Place all ingredients in bowl and gently toss. Keep covered in refrigerator for 1 hour to allow flavours to combine.

FRIED TOMATOES WITH PARMESAN

SERVES 4

2	large tomatoes
3 tablespoons	olive oil
2 tablespoons	basil, finely chopped
	salt and pepper
¼ cup	Parmesan cheese, grated

Slice tomatoes into ¼" rounds and place on paper towel to absorb excess moisture. Season both sides of tomatoes generously with salt and pepper.

Heat olive oil in large skillet on medium high heat. Place tomatoes in hot pan and cook for about 1 minute. Flip over. Sprinkle tops of tomatoes with Parmesan cheese and continue cooking until cheese slightly melts.

Remove tomatoes from pan and finish with fresh chopped basil. Serve immediately.

These tomatoes go beautifully with Perfect Scrambled Eggs (page 60). A hard cheese such as Asiago or aged white cheddar may also be substituted for the Parmesan cheese.

SOFT BOILED EGGS

SERVES 2

4 slices	whole wheat bread
2 tablespoons	butter, softened
2	extra large eggs
	fleur de sel
pinch	cayenne

For traditional soft boiled eggs, fill sauce pan with water ⅔ full and bring to boil over high heat.

Place whole eggs gently into water using slotted spoon and reduce heat to a gentle simmer. Cook eggs for 4 minutes, remove with slotted spoon and submerge under cold running water for 1 minute.

Toast bread until golden brown, spread evenly with softened butter and cut into ¾" strips.

When eggs are cool enough to handle place the egg small end down in an egg cup. Gently crack the egg open using a butter knife and sprinkle a few grains of salt and a small pinch of cayenne over the runny yolk.

Serve immediately with toast and a small spoon for scooping out the egg white from inside the shell.

At Fairholme, we serve soft boiled eggs with our homemade Irish Soda Bread (page 77).

Fleur de Sel: This "flower of salt" is an all-natural sea salt that is harvested by hand in Brittany, France. Other artisan and gourmet sea salts are available in most grocery stores.

POACHED EGGS

SERVES 2

4   large eggs
dash   cayenne

Fill large skillet almost to the brim with cold water. Bring water to boil over high heat and reduce to medium or gentle simmer. Crack eggs one at a time into a small teacup. Pour each egg slowly into the gently simmering water. Allow the whites to start coagulating before dropping in the entire egg. Bring water back up to temperature between each egg.

Allow eggs to lightly simmer in poaching water for 2½-3 minutes or until whites are completely cooked. Remove each egg with a slotted spoon and drain excess liquid. For a perfectly shaped poached egg, carefully trim excess strands off each egg with a clean pair of scissors. These eggs are now ready for assembly in our traditional Eggs Benedict recipe (page 36) or served on their own with toast and a dash of cayenne.

Many people use white vinegar in their egg poaching water to keep the eggs intact. At Fairholme we like to keep the taste of our farm fresh eggs pure so we use the vinegar-free method.

MEDITERRANEAN BISCUITS

MAKES 12 BISCUITS

This is an extremely moist and savoury biscuit recipe. It is a delicious addition to any breakfast or brunch. Best served straight out of the oven.

2 cups	all-purpose flour
2 tablespoons	baking powder
1 tablespoon	sugar
1 tablespoon	basil or green onion, chopped
¼ teaspoon	salt
6 tablespoons	butter, cold
¾ cup	feta cheese, crumbled
3 tablespoons	sundried tomatoes, drained and chopped
1	egg
¾ cup	light cream
	olive oil
	coarse salt

Preheat oven to 400°F.

Sift flour, baking powder, sugar, basil and salt into the bowl of a food processor. Pulse a few times to mix the dry ingredients together. Cut the butter into 1" cubes and add to the processor. Pulse until the mixture resembles coarse peas.

Add feta and sundried tomatoes to dry ingredients in processor. Whisk together egg and cream and slowly pour into the biscuit mix, pulsing after each addition. Be careful not to overmix.

On a lightly floured surface, pat or roll the dough to a 1" thickness. Using a 2" cutter, cut the dough into desired shape and place on parchment-lined baking sheet. Use two baking sheets together to prevent the bottoms of the biscuits from becoming too brown.

Lightly brush the tops with olive oil and sprinkle with coarse salt. Bake 15-20 minutes or until lightly golden.

ASIAGO CORN MUFFINS

MAKES 12 MUFFINS

1 cup	cornmeal
1 cup	all-purpose flour
4 teaspoons	baking powder
½ teaspoon	baking soda
¼ cup	maple syrup
¼ teaspoon	salt
1	large egg, beaten
1¼ cups	buttermilk
¼ cup	vegetable oil
½ cup	Asiago or Fontina cheese, grated
3 tablespoons	fresh thyme, finely chopped

Preheat oven to 375°F.

Spray muffin tins with cooking spray and combine dry ingredients in a bowl. In a separate bowl combine egg, milk, oil and maple syrup, and add to dry ingredients.

Stir until moistened, but don't overwork.

Fill greased tins with batter and sprinkle muffins with cheese and thyme. Bake for 15 minutes.

QUICK RISING BROWN BREAD

MAKES 1 LOAF

2¾ cups	bread flour
1½ cups	wheat bran
½ cup	brown sugar
½ teaspoon	salt
1 teaspoon	baking soda
½ teaspoon	baking powder
2½ cups	apple juice

Sunny's Grandma Ada gave us this wonderful bread recipe. It's a family tradition that never fails!

Preheat oven to 350°F.

Prepare 8" loaf pan with cooking spray. Combine dry ingredients in mixing bowl. Pour in apple juice and stir to combine. Dough should be moist.

Place dough in loaf pan and smooth out to the edges. Bake in oven for 60 minutes or until tester comes out clean. Cool for 10 minutes in pan and turn out onto wire rack. Serve warm with butter and jam.

IRISH SODA BREAD

MAKES 2 LOAVES

2 cups	all-purpose flour
1½ teaspoons	baking powder
½ teaspoon	baking soda
½ teaspoon	salt
1 tablespoon	sugar
6 tablespoons	unsalted butter
1 cup	buttermilk

Preheat oven to 350°F.

Mix flour, baking powder, baking soda, salt and sugar in a food processor. Add pieces of butter and pulse until smooth and no longer lumpy. Pour in buttermilk and pulse until it forms into an elastic-like dough.

Form dough mixture into a round shape and place in buttered baking pan. Bake for 35-40 minutes or until golden on top. Serve warm with butter.

Before baking we brush the dough with olive oil and sprinkle the top with fleur de sel, cracked pepper and fresh, finely chopped herbs. Chives, rosemary or basil may also be used. This is a great brunch addition.

CHEDDAR CHIVE BISCUITS

SERVES 10 – 12

2 cups	all-purpose flour
1 tablespoon	baking powder
1 teaspoon	salt
1¼ cups	unsalted butter, cold
1 cup	cheddar cheese, grated
¼ cup	fresh chives or green onions, finely chopped
1 cup	milk
2 teaspoons	unsalted butter, melted

Preheat oven to 400°F.

Combine flour, baking powder and salt in mixing bowl. Cut butter into flour with pastry cutter until mixture resembles coarse cornmeal. Stir in grated cheese and chopped chives. Add milk and stir with a fork until a soft dough forms. Do not overwork.

Halve the dough and form into two balls. Place each ball on a lightly floured surface and pat down with hands to form rounds of 1" thickness. Cut each round like a pie into 6 pieces. You will end up with 12 scones in total. Place on parchment-lined baking sheet. Use two baking sheets together to prevent the bottoms of the biscuits from becoming too brown.

Brush each biscuit lightly with melted butter. Bake about 15 minutes. Serve fresh from the oven with a little butter.

BAKED RASPBERRY FRENCH TOAST

SERVES 2

This recipe was featured in the May 2002 issue of Glamour magazine.

4 slices	day-old Italian bread, cut into ½" cubes
½ cup	fresh or frozen raspberries or blueberries
2 ounces	cream cheese, cut into ½" cubes
3	eggs
1 cup	milk
1 tablespoon	maple syrup
¼ teaspoon	poppy seeds

If you don't have ramekins, large muffin tins work well. This recipe is ideal for special occasions such as a celebration brunch or romantic breakfast for two. It may be prepared the night before.

The night before:

Grease two 8-ounce ramekins or large muffin tins. Line bottom half of tins with bread cubes. Cover with raspberries or blueberries and cream cheese cubes and top with remaining bread. Mix eggs, milk and syrup and sprinkle with poppy seeds. Pour mixture over bread, cover and let soak overnight in refrigerator.

In the morning:

Bake at 350°F for 25-30 minutes or until puffy and golden. Remove French toast from ramekins and top with Berry Compote or Lemon Sauce (page 82).

BERRY COMPOTE

zest and juice	1 lemon
1 tablespoon	water
4 cups	fresh or frozen berries
1 tablespoon	maple syrup
⅛ teaspoon	cinnamon

Combine all ingredients in a saucepan and simmer over medium heat until berries begin to break down and sauce starts to thicken. Serve over French toast.

LEMON SAUCE

1	egg
¾ cup	sugar
4 tablespoons	lemon juice
zest	1 large lemon
1 tablespoon	butter

Whisk together first four ingredients and cook over low heat, stirring constantly. After sauce begins to thicken, stir in butter just to combine. Serve warm over French toast as an alternative to the berry compote.

APPLE PUFF

SERVES 4

2	Granny Smith apples
4	large eggs
¼ cup	butter
½ cup	all-purpose flour, sifted
½ cup	milk
1 teaspoon	pure vanilla
dash	salt
	raw sugar

Preheat oven to 450°F.

Generously butter one glass pie dish. Cut butter into cubes and place in bottom of dish. Peel, quarter and thinly slice apples. Layer in bottom of dish and microwave for 5 minutes.

Beat eggs with hand beater. Add flour to make a thick paste and then add milk, vanilla and salt. Pour egg mixture over the apples and bake for 10 minutes (the high temperature allows the mixture to puff up).

Remove from oven and sprinkle with raw sugar. Cut into four pieces and serve with crisp bacon.

FAIRHOLME WAFFLES

SERVES 4

1¾ cups	all-purpose flour
2 teaspoons	baking powder
½ teaspoon	salt
1 tablespoon	sugar
3	eggs, separated
5 tablespoons	butter, melted
1½ cups	milk
1 teaspoon	pure vanilla

Waffles are a fun buffet brunch item. Set out bowls of various toppings such as whipped cream, fresh berries, bananas, chocolate sauce or even ice cream. Create your own breakfast delight!

Preheat waffle iron and grease lightly with cooking spray.

Sift together flour, baking powder, salt and sugar into large bowl. Combine egg yolks, melted butter, milk and vanilla in a separate bowl.

Add wet ingredients into dry and gently fold together until just moistened. Do not overwork. Batter should have a slightly pebbled look, similar to a muffin batter.

Beat 3 egg whites until stiff and lightly fold into the batter.

Pour ¾ cup batter into preheated waffle iron and cook until steam stops, about 4 to 5 minutes. Topping options include whipped cream, a dash of cinnamon, powdered sugar and maple syrup.

CHOCOLATE LOVER'S WAFFLES WITH RASPBERRY SYRUP

SERVES 4

These waffles look scrumptious on a plate served with whipped cream and fresh berries. They are perfect for a romantic morning. Breakfast in bed?

2 cups	all-purpose flour
¼ cup	cocoa powder
2 tablespoons	sugar
1 tablespoon	baking powder
dash	salt
2	eggs, beaten
¼ cup	melted butter
2 cups	milk
2 teaspoons	pure vanilla

Preheat waffle iron and grease lightly with cooking spray.

Sift together flour, cocoa powder, sugar, baking powder and salt into large bowl. Combine eggs, melted butter, milk and vanilla in a separate bowl.

Add wet ingredients into dry and gently fold together until just moistened. Do not overwork. Batter should have a slightly pebbled look, similar to a muffin batter.

Pour ¾ cup batter into preheated waffle iron and cook until steam stops, about 4 to 5 minutes. Topping options include fresh raspberry syrup, maple syrup and powdered sugar.

Raspberry or Strawberry Syrup

½ cup	water
½ cup	sugar
1 pound	fresh or frozen raspberries or strawberries
1 tablespoon	fresh lemon juice

Simmer water, lemon juice and sugar in saucepan until sugar is dissolved. Add berries and cook for a few minutes until liquid is reduced and sauce-like consistency is reached.

Pour mixture into blender. Blend until you have a lovely smooth purée and pass through strainer to remove seeds.

OVEN BAKED PECAN FRENCH TOAST

SERVES 8

8	1½" slices French bread or other thickly sliced bread
¼ cup	butter, melted
¼ cup	maple syrup
¾ cup	pecans, chopped
8	eggs
2½ cups	milk
1 teaspoon	pure vanilla
1 teaspoon	cinnamon
pinch	nutmeg
zest	1 orange (optional)
pinch	salt

This is another delicious breakfast dish that can be prepared the night before. The French toast has a rich, custard-like texture and taste.

Preheat oven to 375°F.

Combine melted butter and maple syrup. Pour into large, deep cookie sheet or baking pan. Sprinkle with chopped pecans.

Mix together the eggs, milk, vanilla, cinnamon, nutmeg, orange zest and salt. Soak bread slices in the egg mixture until saturated. Place in pan on top of maple syrup mixture.

Pour any remaining egg mixture over the bread. Sprinkle with more chopped pecans. Cover tightly and place in refrigerator overnight.

Bake for 30 minutes or until golden and puffy. Serve with warm maple syrup and powdered sugar.

DEEP DISH BLUEBERRY VANILLA FRENCH TOAST

SERVES 12 – 14

2 loaves	Italian bread
8 ounces	cream cheese
1½ cups	blueberries, fresh or frozen
12	eggs
¼ cup	maple syrup
2½ cups	light cream
1 tablespoon	pure vanilla
1 teaspoon	cinnamon

This dish is best made the night before.

Grease a 9"x13" baking dish with butter. Remove crust from loaves and cut loaves in half lengthwise.

In a mixing bowl, blend 1 cup blueberries and cream cheese. Spread the cream cheese mixture on both sides of the bread and put halves together to form a sandwich. Cut loaves into 1" cubes.

In a large mixing bowl whisk together eggs, maple syrup, cream, vanilla and cinnamon. Put bread cubes in prepared baking dish and pour egg mixture over the cubes. Press bread down gently to flatten. Sprinkle remaining blueberries over top. Cover and refrigerate overnight.

In the morning preheat oven to 350°F.

Cook for 55-60 minutes or until puffy and golden. Cut into portions and serve warm with crème fraîche (page 100), maple syrup or lemon sauce (page 82).

LEMON SCONES

MAKES 12 SCONES

3 cups	all-purpose flour
3 tablespoons	sugar
2 tablespoons	baking powder
¼ teaspoon	salt
zest	1 lemon
¾ cup	cold butter
1	egg
	buttermilk
¼ cup	currants (optional)
	raw sugar

Serve scones with crème fraîche and fruit jam. Fabulous for loved ones and special occasions.

Preheat oven to 375°F.

Sift flour, sugar, baking powder, salt and the lemon zest into the bowl of a food processor. Pulse a few times to mix the dry ingredients.

Cut the butter into 1" cubes and add to the processor. Pulse until the mixture resembles coarse peas. Crack the egg into a large glass measuring cup and beat lightly. Add the buttermilk until the liquid reaches 9 ounces.

Slowly add the liquid to the batter, pulsing after each addition. Be careful not to overmix. Only pulse until the mixture starts to come together.

Turn out dough on a lightly floured surface. If using currants, add them now. Pat or roll the dough to a 1" thickness. Using a 2" cutter (we like to use heart-shaped cutters), cut the dough into desired shape and place on parchment-lined baking sheet. Use two baking sheets together to prevent the bottoms of the scones from becoming too brown.

Sprinkle the top with raw sugar. Bake about 15 minutes until lightly golden.

Sprinkle lightly with powdered sugar before serving.

SCONE VARIATIONS

Apricot Almond Scones

Make the scone base on page 95, omitting the lemon zest. Cut in ½ cup diced dried apricots. Cut out scones, sprinkle with sliced almonds and raw, coarse sugar. Sprinkle lightly with powdered sugar before serving.

White Chocolate, Cranberry and Orange Scones

Make the scone base on page 95, substituting 1 teaspoon orange zest instead of lemon. Add ¾ cup white chocolate chips and ½ cup dried cranberries. Sprinkle lightly with powdered sugar before serving.

Sugar Berry Scones

Make the scone base on page 95. Add approximately ½ cup fresh or frozen berries and sprinkle with raw, coarse sugar. Sprinkle lightly with powdered sugar before serving.

PUMPKIN SCONES WITH ORANGE GLAZE

MAKES 12 SCONES

3 cups	all-purpose flour
3 tablespoons	brown sugar
2 tablespoons	baking powder
¼ teaspoon	salt
1 teaspoon	ground ginger
1½ teaspoons	cinnamon
¾ cup	cold butter
1	egg
⅓ cup	buttermilk
1 teaspoon	pure vanilla
¾ cup	canned pumpkin
½ cup	dried cranberries

Preheat oven to 400°F.

Sift flour, brown sugar, baking powder, salt and spices into the bowl of a food processor. Pulse a few times to mix together the dry ingredients.

Cut the butter into 1" cubes and add to the processor. Pulse until the mixture resembles coarse peas.

Combine egg, buttermilk, vanilla and pumpkin. Add the liquid slowly to the scone mix, pulsing after each addition. Be careful not to overmix.

Halve the dough and form into two balls. Place each ball on a lightly floured surface and pat down with hands to form rounds of 1" thickness. Cut each round like a pie into 6 pieces. You will end up with 12 scones in total. Place on parchment-lined baking sheet. Use two baking sheets together to prevent the bottoms of the scones from becoming too brown.

Sprinkle the tops with raw sugar. As an alternative you can also cover the scones with a glaze after baking.

Bake for 20-25 minutes or until golden.

Orange Glaze

2 tablespoons	butter
2 cups	powdered sugar
2 tablespoons	fresh orange juice

Heat ingredients in double boiler. Whisk until butter and sugar are melted and glaze has slightly thickened. Remove from heat, beat until smooth and allow to semi-cool. Drizzle glaze over scones and let harden slightly.

CRÈME FRAÎCHE

1½ cups   whipping cream
½ cup   buttermilk

Mix together the whipping cream and buttermilk in a clean container.

Let stand at room temperature loosely covered for about 16 hours. Refrigerate until crème fraîche reaches desired thickness. The crème fraîche will continue to firm up in the refrigerator.

You can thin out your crème fraîche by whisking it in a small bowl or adding a splash more whipping cream. Delicious with scones, waffles, French toast or smoked fish. It is a lighter alternative to heavy Devonshire cream and just as tasty.

RASPBERRY BUTTER

½ cup   fresh or frozen raspberries
¼ cup   powdered sugar
1 cup   butter, room temperature

In a small saucepan over low heat, combine the berries and powdered sugar until softened.

Remove from heat and let cool.

Add butter and mix until combined. This may take a few minutes, but it will come together.

Cover and refrigerate until ready to serve. Delicious with warm scones.

Special Butters: Flavoured butters are so tasty and only take a few minutes to prepare. Create your own combinations with whatever ingredients you have on hand. Flavoured butters also freeze well.

CINNAMON MAPLE BUTTER

1 cup	butter, room temperature
4 tablespoons	maple syrup
1 tablespoon	cinnamon

Soften butter to room temperature. Place butter, maple syrup and cinnamon in mixing bowl. Mix until light and fluffy. Serve at room temperature.

TOASTED PECAN, ORANGE AND BROWN SUGAR BUTTER

1 cup	butter, room temperature
1 cup	packed brown sugar
1 tablespoon	cinnamon
½ cup	lightly toasted pecans
zest	1 orange

Preheat oven to 325°F.

Place pecans in one layer on baking sheet and toast about 6 minutes or until golden and slightly fragrant. Let cool. Chop pecans into small pieces.

In mixing bowl place softened butter, brown sugar, cinnamon, pecans and orange zest. Mix until light and fluffy.

Serve at room temperature with toast, scones, pancakes or French toast.

CINNAMON APPLES IN PHYLLO PASTRY

SERVES 8

3	Granny Smith apples
½ cup	white sugar
1 tablespoon	cinnamon
juice	½ lemon
pinch	nutmeg
4 full sheets	phyllo pastry
½ cup	unsalted butter, melted

Topping

¼ cup	brown sugar
¼ cup	sliced almonds
¼ cup	raisins
	whipping cream

A nice option for brunch is to make these as individual apple kisses. Cut the phyllo sheets into 6 squares. Top each square with ¼ cup of the cinnamon apple mix. Bring opposite corners of the phyllo together at the top to form little pouches or kisses.

Preheat oven to 375°F.

Peel and slice apples into thin wedges of equal thickness, place in mixing bowl and toss with white sugar, cinnamon, lemon and nutmeg. Set aside.

Cover large baking sheet with parchment paper. Use two baking sheets together to prevent the bottom of the phyllo from becoming too brown when baking.

Place one piece of phyllo on tray. Using pastry brush, spread melted butter over the entire sheet. Place second piece of phyllo directly on top of first piece and brush with butter. Repeat with remaining phyllo.

Place apples slices one at a time on phyllo to form two uniform rows, leaving a 3" border around the edges. Sprinkle apples with brown sugar, sliced almonds and raisins. Starting with the ends, fold phyllo twice toward the apples to form edges. Repeat with sides. Make sure the folded edges are higher than the apples to prevent juices from leaking out. Brush edges of phyllo with remaining butter and bake until phyllo is golden brown all over. Make sure it's fully cooked, about 20 minutes.

Cut into strips widthwise and serve warm with whipped cream and powdered sugar.

SWEET MASCARPONE AND STRAWBERRY LEMON TURNOVER

SERVES 9

6 sheets	phyllo pastry
½ cup	unsalted butter, melted
¼ cup	sugar
1 cup	strawberry jam
1 teaspoon	lemon zest
1 cup	mascarpone
	fresh berries for garnish

Preheat oven to 375°F.

Cut phyllo widthwise into three stacks to make 18 strips. Cover phyllo with slightly dampened tea towel to prevent from drying out. Mix lemon zest into strawberry jam.

For each turnover take one piece of phyllo and brush generously with melted butter. Sprinkle with white sugar. Place a second strip of phyllo on top of the first and brush with more butter. Put a tablespoon of mascarpone ½" above the bottom corner and place a generous spoonful of jam over mascarpone.

Fold phyllo on the diagonal to form a small triangle pocket. Continue folding to end of phyllo strip. Place triangle pocket seam side down on parchment-lined baking sheet. Use two baking sheets together to prevent the bottom of the phyllo from becoming too brown when baking.

Brush top of phyllo with remaining butter. Bake for 20 minutes until phyllo is fully cooked and golden brown. Serve warm with fresh berries and powdered sugar.

Mascarpone is a soft, mild Italian specialty cheese that is a delicious accompaniment with any fresh fruit.

Substitute different jams or marmalade for the strawberry jam. These turnovers can be made a day ahead and kept in the refrigerator. Simply bake before serving.

FAIRHOLME'S BERRY MUFFINS

MAKES 12 MUFFINS

2 cups	quick oats
1½ cups	all-purpose flour
2 teaspoons	baking powder
2 teaspoons	cinnamon
dash	allspice
½ cup	sunflower oil
2	eggs
1 teaspoon	pure vanilla
¾ cup	brown sugar
1 cup	buttermilk or vanilla yogurt
1 cup	fresh or frozen berries

Optional Streusel Topping

¼ cup	brown sugar
¼ cup	all-purpose flour
¼ cup	quick oats
¼ cup	unsalted butter, cold

Preheat oven to 350°F.

Prepare muffin tins with cooking spray. Make streusel topping by cutting butter into dry ingredients until fully mixed and crumbly. Set aside.

Mix together quick oats, flour, baking powder, cinnamon and allspice in medium bowl. In a separate bowl combine oil, eggs, vanilla, brown sugar and buttermilk. Add to dry ingredients until just combined. Do not overmix.

Fill muffin tins half full and top each with berries. Scoop the remaining batter on top of the berries. Sprinkle streusel topping over muffin batter before baking.

Bake muffins 25-30 minutes or until tester comes out clean and muffins are golden brown. Allow muffins to cool in tins for 5 minutes before removing them to racks. Serve warm with butter and jam.

FAIRHOLME'S MORNING GLORY MUFFINS

MAKES 12 MUFFINS

This is a classic muffin that is both moist and satisfying. Don't let grating carrots scare you away and always throw in an extra dash of cinnamon.

2 cups	all-purpose flour
1 cup	sugar
2 teaspoons	baking soda
1 tablespoon	cinnamon
½ teaspoon	allspice
pinch	nutmeg
½ teaspoon	salt
½ cup	shredded coconut
½ cup	raisins
2 cups	carrots, grated
1	apple, peeled and grated
1 cup	crushed pineapple, drained
½ cup	pecans or walnuts, chopped
3	eggs
⅔ cup	vegetable oil
1 teaspoon	pure vanilla

Preheat oven to 350°F.

Prepare muffin tins with cooking spray. In a large bowl sift together the flour, sugar, baking soda, cinnamon, allspice, nutmeg and salt. Add the coconut, raisins, carrot, apple, pineapple and nuts.

In a separate bowl mix the eggs, vegetable oil and vanilla. Pour the liquid into the dry ingredients and stir until just combined. Divide into prepared muffin tins and bake for 25-30 minutes. Allow the muffins to cool in tins for 5 minutes before removing them to racks.

CRANBERRY CORNMEAL MUFFINS

MAKES 16 MUFFINS

3	large eggs
1⅔ cups	vegetable oil
1⅔ cups	buttermilk
¼ cup	honey
½ cup	cornmeal
1 tablespoon	lemon zest or orange zest
4½ cups	all-purpose flour
1 cup	sugar
1½ tablespoons	baking powder
1¼ teaspoons	baking soda
1¼ teaspoons	salt
1½ cups	fresh or frozen cranberries

Topping

½ cup	cornmeal
½ cup	brown sugar
2 tablespoons	unsalted butter, melted

Preheat oven to 350°F.

Prepare muffin tins with cooking spray. Mix together cornmeal, brown sugar and butter for topping. Set aside.

In large mixing bowl stir together dry ingredients. In separate bowl mix together wet ingredients. Add wet ingredients to dry mixture and fold together until moistened. Do not overwork.

Gently fold berries into batter and fill prepared muffins tins three-quarters full. Sprinkle topping over each muffin and bake 25-30 minutes or until tester comes out clean.

BANANA GRANOLA MUFFINS

MAKES 16 MUFFINS

We use our delicious Fairholme Granola in this recipe – it's a morning favourite!

3 cups	all-purpose flour
¾ cup	sugar
2 teaspoons	baking powder
1 teaspoon	baking soda
½ teaspoon	salt
1 cup	butter, melted
2	large eggs
¾ cup	milk
2 teaspoons	pure vanilla
2	ripe medium bananas, mashed
1	medium banana, diced
1½ cups	granola
	pecan halves for topping

Preheat oven to 350°F.

Prepare large muffin tins with cooking spray. Sift flour, sugar, baking powder, baking soda and salt into a large mixing bowl.

Combine butter, eggs, milk, vanilla and mashed bananas in a blender until smooth. Gently fold batter into dry ingredients without overmixing. Fold in diced banana and granola.

Scoop mixture into prepared muffin tins and place a pecan half on top of each. For a sweeter, crunchier taste we often sprinkle a little raw sugar on top of the muffin mix.

Bake for 25 minutes or until golden brown. Leave in tins for 5 minutes and then remove and allow to cool on racks.

ORANGE YOGURT MUFFINS

MAKES 12 MUFFINS

1	large orange, peeled
1	egg
¼ cup	oil
¾ cup	yogurt, plain or French vanilla
1 teaspoon	pure vanilla
1¼ cups	all-purpose flour
½ cup	wheat germ
½ cup	brown sugar
1 tablespoon	baking powder
1 teaspoon	baking soda
pinch	salt
½ cup	raisins or currants
¼ cup	sliced almonds

Preheat oven to 350°F.

Prepare muffin tins with cooking spray. In large mixing bowl thoroughly combine flour, wheat germ, brown sugar, baking powder, baking soda and salt.

Place orange in blender and blend for 30 seconds. Transfer to separate mixing bowl with egg, oil, yogurt and vanilla. Mix thoroughly. Make a well in the centre of the dry ingredients. Pour wet mixture into well and fold gently just to moisten. Do not overmix.

Fold in raisins and nuts. Fill prepared muffin tins with batter. Bake for 20-25 minutes or until golden brown. Let muffins cool in tins for 5 minutes, remove and cool on racks. Serve with butter.

These moist muffins freeze extremely well.

Buttermilk may be used as a substitute for the yogurt.

LEMON LAVENDER BLUEBERRY MUFFINS

MAKES 12 LARGE MUFFINS

1½ cups	sugar
½ cup	butter, very soft
2	eggs
1½ cups	buttermilk
2 teaspoons	lemon zest
3½ cups	all-purpose flour
4 teaspoons	baking powder
½ teaspoon	salt
1 teaspoon	lavender flowers, fresh or dried
3 cups	fresh or frozen blueberries

Crumble Topping

1 cup	brown sugar
⅔ cup	all-purpose flour
½ cup	butter
2 teaspoons	lemon zest
1 teaspoon	lavender flowers

Preheat oven to 350°F.

Prepare 12 large muffin tins with cooking spray. Using your hands, mix together crumble topping ingredients. Set aside.

Whisk together sugar and butter until combined and then whisk in the eggs, buttermilk and lemon zest.

Sift dry ingredients on top of the wet ingredients and gently fold together without overmixing. Fold in blueberries and lavender flowers. Divide muffin batter into muffin tins and sprinkle crumble topping over the top.

Bake muffins 25-30 minutes or until tester comes out clean and muffins are golden. Let muffins cool in tins for 5 minutes, remove and cool on racks.

CRUNCHY RASPBERRY BLACKBERRY MUFFINS

MAKES 16 – 18 MUFFINS

3 cups	all-purpose flour
1½ cups	sugar
1 tablespoon	baking powder
½ teaspoon	baking soda
½ teaspoon	salt
1 tablespoon	cinnamon
1¼ cups	whole milk
2	extra large eggs, lightly beaten
1 cup	unsalted butter, melted
1 cup	fresh or frozen raspberries
1 cup	fresh or frozen blackberries
¼ cup	raw sugar

Kids love these colourful, delicious muffins.

Preheat oven to 375°F.

Spray muffin tins lightly with cooking spray.

Sift together flour, sugar, baking powder, baking soda, salt and cinnamon in large mixing bowl. In separate bowl combine milk, eggs and melted butter. Make a well in the centre of the dry ingredients and pour wet ingredients into well. Gently fold together muffin batter without overmixing.

Gently fold in raspberries and blackberries. Scoop batter into prepared tins and sprinkle muffins with raw sugar. Bake 25-30 minutes or until tester comes out clean. Muffins should be golden. Let muffins cool in tins for 5 minutes, remove and cool on racks.

MAPLE BANANA LOAF WITH PECANS

MAKES 1 LARGE LOAF

2¾ cups	all-purpose flour
2 teaspoons	baking soda
2 teaspoons	baking powder
½ teaspoon	salt
½ cup	unsalted butter, room temperature
¾ cup	white sugar
½ cup	brown sugar
3	large eggs
3	large bananas, well ripened
¼ cup	buttermilk
¼ cup	maple syrup
½ cup	pecans, chopped and toasted

We often make a few loaves at a time because they freeze so nicely. It's the perfect treat for unexpected guests.

Preheat oven to 350°F.

Grease a 9"x5" loaf pan. In mixer cream together butter, white sugar and brown sugar. Scrape down sides of mixing bowl. Add eggs one at a time until fully incorporated. In a separate bowl combine flour, baking soda, baking powder and salt. In another bowl, mash bananas with buttermilk and maple syrup.

On low speed add half the flour mixture to the egg mixture until just combined. Fold in the banana purée. Add remaining flour. Do not overmix the batter.

Using a spatula, fold in toasted pecans. Place batter in greased loaf pan and tap down gently on counter to even out mixture. Bake 50-60 minutes or until tester comes out clean. Cool in pan for 10 minutes and then turn out onto wire rack.

ZUCCHINI, PECAN AND CHOCOLATE BREAKFAST CAKE

MAKES 2 LOAVES

3	eggs
2 cups	sugar
2 teaspoons	pure vanilla
1 cup	vegetable oil
1 cup	pumpkin purée
2 cups	zucchini, grated
3 cups	all-purpose flour
1 teaspoon	baking powder
1 teaspoon	baking soda
1 teaspoon	salt
1 teaspoon	cinnamon
1 cup	chocolate chips
1 cup	pecans, chopped

Preheat oven to 350°F.

Grease two loaf pans. In mixing bowl beat eggs and sugar on high until fluffy and light in colour. In separate bowl mix vanilla, oil, pumpkin purée and zucchini. In another bowl combine flour, baking powder, baking soda, salt and cinnamon.

With mixer on low, alternate adding dry and wet mixtures until thoroughly combined. Do not overmix. Fold in chocolate chips and pecans.

Divide mixture between pans and tap down gently on counter to even out mixture. Bake for 50-60 minutes or until tester comes out clean.

Cool in pan for 10 minutes and then turn out onto wire rack.

LEMON BLUEBERRY LOAF WITH LEMON SUGAR GLAZE

MAKES 2 LOAVES

1 cup	unsalted butter, room temperature
2 cups	sugar
5	eggs
3 cups	all-purpose flour
½ teaspoon	baking powder
½ teaspoon	baking soda
1 teaspoon	salt
¾ cup	buttermilk
1 cup	fresh or frozen blueberries
½ cup	lemon juice
¼ cup	lemon zest

Preheat oven to 350°F.

Grease two loaf pans. Cream together butter and sugar in mixer until fluffy and pale in colour. Add eggs one at a time, scraping down sides until eggs are fully incorporated.

Sift together flour, baking powder, baking soda and salt. In a separate bowl mix buttermilk, lemon juice and zest. With mixer on low speed, alternate dry and wet ingredients, ending with dry. Do not overmix. Add blueberries and fold in gently.

Divide mix between two loaf pans and tap down gently on counter to even out mixture. Put loaf pans on baking sheet with space between them and place on middle rack of oven. Bake for 1 hour or until tester comes out clean. Cool for 10 minutes, invert and place on wire rack. Top loaves with Lemon Sugar Glaze.

Lemon Sugar Glaze

2 cups	powdered sugar
2 tablespoons	fresh lemon juice, strained

In mixing bowl combine powdered sugar and lemon juice. Whisk together until smooth. Pour over tops of loaves while they are still slightly warm. Let glaze set.

This loaf is moist and freezes well. Take it out the night before and simply add the glaze before your guests arrive.

Contributors

Sunny Dinney
Fairholme Chef

Sunny Dinney adds an elegant flair to the breakfasts and brunches served at Fairholme. She pairs fresh, locally produced foods with simple cooking techniques. The result is a memorable meal that complements the beauty and unique style of Fairholme Manor. Sunny has been in the hospitality industry since 1996 and trained under Chef de Cuisine Erik Andersen at Camosun College. She and Sylvia work together as a dynamic team to create delicious breakfasts and brunches for Fairholme's guests.

sunnydinney@gmail.com

Sue Frause
Editor

Sue Frause is an award-winning freelance writer and photographer. Her articles and images have appeared in *The Daily Herald*, *The Province*, *Northwest Palate* and numerous other print and online publications. She also writes a travel blog (*Sue's Road Notes*) and a blog for the *Seattle Post-Intelligencer*. Sue and her husband Bob live on Whidbey Island where they tend to their garden, chickens and very own field of dreams.

www.suefrause.com

John Archer of John Archer Photography
Cover, Food and Inn Photography

John Archer is a photographer based in Victoria, BC, specializing in wedding photography for the past 15 years. His style is a combination of photojournalism and glamour/fashion photography.

www.archerphotography.com

Cathie Ferguson of Infocus Photographic
Additional Photography of Inn and Gardens

Cathie Ferguson has been a Victoria-based photographer for the past ten years, specializing in commercial and portrait work. She has travelled extensively and especially enjoys photographing interiors and architecture. "I really enjoy working with people to capture the beauty in the spaces they have created. It is a very rewarding aspect of being a photographer."

cathieferguson@gmail.com

Susan Ramsey of Ramsey & Ramsey
Flower Designer

Susan Ramsey has been the exclusive florist for the Fairmont Empress Hotel for 10 years and was the floral designer for Queen Elizabeth II during her visit to Victoria in 2002. She was the lead floral designer for the BC Pavilion at Expo '86 and designed the flowers for Princess Diana's visit. Susan has been in business for more than 30 years and is a weekly garden columnist for the *Times-Colonist*.

www.ramseyflowers.com

Jill Louise Campbell
Artist

Artist Jill Louise Campbell paints with a palette as rich in whimsy as colour. The architecture and ambiance of Fairholme Manor has inspired her over the years, a series of 5 paintings have resulted capturing the romance of this Victorian treasure. Jill Louise Campbell Fine Art Gallery is located in the heart of Ganges, Salt Spring Island. This personal gallery is home to her reproductions from giclée to art cards and originals.

www.jlcgallery.com

Inge Ranzinger of BoardWalk Designs
Artist

Although always passionate about art, Inge began painting seriously about six years ago. Her medium is acrylic and mixed media on canvas. Several of her paintings are at Fairholme Manor. Inge has a background in advertising design, museum display and currently works as an interior designer. She studied art at Victoria's Camosun College and has worked with some of Victoria's finest painters. Inge is a juried artist and has displayed at the Sooke Art Show and many local galleries.

www.members.shaw.ca/ingeran

Additional Artwork at Fairholme by Pat Potvin and Kristine Paton

Pat Potvin is a longtime member of the Victoria Sketch Club and belongs to the Federation of Canadian Artists. Her work has been favourably received and hangs in private collections across Canada, the USA, Europe and South Africa. genep@shaw.ca

Kristine Paton has been a professional artist for more than 16 years. A former member of the Federation of Canadian Artists, her work is shown worldwide in private and corporate collections. In British Columbia, her paintings are exhibited at galleries in Shawnigan Lake, White Rock and Kelowna. www.paton-place.com.

Index

We hope you've enjoyed your visit to *Fabulous Fairholme!*